better together*

*This book is best read together, grownup and kid.

 akidsco.com

a
kids
book
about

a kids book about

CONFIDENCE

by Joy Cho

A Kids Co.
Editor Denise Morales Soto
Designer Gabby Nguyen
Creative Director Rick DeLucco
Studio Manager Kenya Feldes
Sales Director Melanie Wilkins
Head of Books Jennifer Goldstein
CEO and Founder Jelani Memory

DK
Editor Emma Roberts
Senior Production Editor Jennifer Murray
Senior Production Controller Louise Minihane
Senior Acquisitions Editor Katy Flint
Managing Art Editor Vicky Short
Publishing Director Mark Searle

This American Edition, 2024
Published in the United States by DK Publishing
1745 Broadway, 20th Floor, New York, NY 10019

DK, a Division of Penguin Random House LLC
Text and design copyright © 2022 by A Kids Book About, Inc.
A Kids Book About, Kids Are Ready, and the colophon 'a' are trademarks of A Kids Book About, Inc.
23 24 25 26 27 10 9 8 7 6 5 4 3 2 1
001-339154-March/2024

A catalog record for this book is available from the Library of Congress.
ISBN: 978-0-7440-9469-5

DK books are available at special discounts when purchased in bulk for
sales promotions, premiums, fund-raising, or educational use. For details, contact:
DK Publishing Special Markets, 1745 Broadway, 20th Floor, New York, NY 10019, or SpecialSales@dk.com

Printed and bound in China

www.dk.com

akidsco.com

MIX
Paper | Supporting
responsible forestry
FSC™ C018179

This book was made with Forest
Stewardship Council™ certified
paper - one small step in DK's
commitment to a sustainable future.
**For more information go to
www.dk.com/our-green-pledge**

To all the kids out there who
want to achieve big things.

And to my daughters—Ruby and Coco—may
you always remember that it's OK to stumble.
It's how you get back up again that matters.

Intro
for grownups

Confidence is something that pretty much every adult I know has trouble with. So how can we expect our kids to be any different? Your kids will go through ups and downs in every phase of life—and every single day. Just like feeling sad or happy, they can feel confident one moment and not confident the next.

My goal for this book is to help explain confidence to kids and help them understand how to empower themselves whenever they need it. Because confident kids (and grownups!) can change the world.

HI!
MY NAME IS JOY.

I'm here to tell you about

CONFIDENCE.

Do you know what being confident means or what confidence feels like?

NOT SURE?

Well, I'm here to help.
By the end of this book,
I hope you'll understand
confidence a little better.

ARE YOU READY?

If the answer is **YES,**
then just turn the page.

DENCE

is believing in yourself
and the things you can do.

It's not something you always have or always don't have.

Some days, you'll feel confident...

and some days, you won't.

When you're confident,
you might feel like you can
and do something

BIG AND
GREAT.

When you don't feel confident, you might feel **small, or sad, or lonely**.

CONFIDENCE ISN'T EASY.

In fact, even grownups
like me have a hard time
with their confidence.

Have you ever wished
you had more of it?

I know I feel that way too, sometimes.

Back when I was in 3rd grade, I moved to a new school in a new town.

I didn't know anyone.

I was the smallest and weakest kid in my class and had to take gym class twice a day to catch up to everyone else. **TWICE!**

I didn't like the same things everyone else did.

I was into art and crafting, and everyone else was into sports or dress-up.

My hair and skin color were not the same as everyone else's, so I was afraid of what other people thought of me.

I was super shy and didn't want to talk to other kids or to my teachers.

All of those things made
me feel insecure.*

And for the very first time, I realized
I didn't have much confidence.

*Insecure means feeling anxious or scared because
 you don't feel sure about yourself.

I wanted to try new things, but by the time I was in 6th grade, I could tell that not being confident was holding me back.

So, one day, I asked my parents if I could try karate—and they said yes!

I started off as a beginner,* which means I had a lot to learn.

*In karate, beginners start at a level called the white belt.

WEEK BY WEEK...

I got

BETTER, STRONGER, AND MORE CONFIDENT

in my skills.

This also changed the way I felt at school and with my friends.

Slowly, I became more confident in other parts of my life.

By the time I finished high school, I had my second-degree black belt* and was good enough to teach other kids and grownups.

*A black belt is the highest level of expertise in karate.

KARATE
CHANGED MY LIFE.

I started a new thing, practiced and got good at it, and didn't let anything hold me back.

It felt good to find what was right for me.

I finally felt OK not being like everyone else.

I HAD FOUND MY CONFIDENCE!

Now, that's not to say
I feel 100% confident every day.
Confidence is always changing.

IT GOES UP...
AND GOES DOWN.

In other words, we can feel confident about something one day, and not confident about that same thing another day.

That's OK. Everyone feels that way.

SO, YOU MIGHT BE ASKING YOURSELF...

How do I get confidence?

What do I do when I am not feeling confident?

Can someone else help me be confident?

That's the tricky part.

The key to gaining confidence is to focus on

WHAT MAKES YOU FEEL GOOD ABOUT YOURSELF.

You lose confidence when you care too much about what other people think.

(I'VE DONE THAT A LOT OF TIMES!)

And you can gain confidence
when other people believe in you.

IT'S A BALANCE.

But...

YOU HAVE TO BELIEVE IN AND TRUST YOURSELF

for it to really work.

Here's something you can do right now, if you're up for it! Grab a pencil and a piece of paper. Then write or draw your answers* to these questions...

WHAT IS 1 THING YOU FEEL CONFIDENT ABOUT RIGHT NOW?

*Maybe your grownup will want to write down their own answers too!

WHAT IS 1 THING YOU DON'T FEEL CONFIDENT ABOUT RIGHT NOW?

Tuck the paper inside these pages, and the next time you come back to read the book, add to your list and see how much it changes.

Here are some things I found helpful when I was learning to find my confidence...

THINK OF SOMETHING YOU WANT TO DO, BUT DON'T FEEL CONFIDENT ABOUT.

LEARN ABOUT IT.

While not feeling confident about something can be hard, knowing more about the thing you want to do can help you feel more confident.

Let's say you want to learn more about drawing. You can read books, watch videos or TV shows about it, take a class, or ask someone for help.

PRACTICE!

When we face our fears,
we gain more confidence.

Maybe you get nervous talking in front of your class. Try making a pretend presentation about anything—like your favorite fruit.

Then, practice sharing it with your family.

HAVE FUN WITH IT!

It doesn't have to be serious! This is about taking small steps toward more confidence.

Maybe you really want to dance with your friends, but don't feel ready yet. Try practicing at home first. Keep it loose, just for fun!

TRY SOMETHING BRAND NEW!

Maybe you could try some spicy food or wear a color you'd normally never pick.

It might be scary to do something you've never done before. But, it can be really exciting too!

Trying new things helps you learn what IS for you and what is NOT for you, all so you can understand yourself more and more.

FIND PEOPLE WHO BELIEVE IN YOU!

Good friends don't make fun of you or make you feel bad about yourself.

Surround yourself with kind, honest, and supportive people who encourage and believe in you.

(CAN YOU THINK OF SOMEONE LIKE THAT?)

And most importantly...

BELIEVE IN

I know it can be hard to believe in yourself, but think back to a time when you worked on something and made progress!

Remember how you felt?
You can do that **AGAIN**
AND AGAIN
AND AGAIN
AND AGAIN.

Confidence isn't always going to be easy. There will be days you feel on top of the world, and days you won't.

But I promise it will get easier to grow your confidence.

Confidence is knowing what's right for **YOU** and not worrying about what other people think.

Once you understand that and work to build your confidence little by little...

NOTHING CAN STOP YOU!

Outro
for grownups

OK, so where do we go from here? As we now know, a lack of confidence isn't an immediately solvable problem. It's an ongoing work-in-progress. But, as parents or caregivers, you can be there to guide kids when they need it. The key to confidence-building for kids is that they have to do the learning and growing mostly alone. Praising them isn't a bad thing, but they gain confidence when they are equipped with new skills, courage, and determination that help them achieve something on their own. And, support them when they discover that a situation, group of friends, or habit is NOT right for them.

You can be there to answer questions, help them learn, and encourage them as needed. And together, we can equip them with the ultimate superpower—confidence in themselves!

About The Author

Joy Cho (she/her) is a Thai American designer, author, and entrepreneur who struggled with confidence a lot as a kid. She was always super shy and didn't know where she could shine.

Now, as a parent to 2 daughters, she recognizes the importance of confidence in every young person's life, as well as the importance of knowing they are not alone. Joy wrote this book for the kid version of herself and for all the kids out there who feel unsure of themselves sometimes and need a little help getting through those moments.

 @ohjoy   @ohjoy

Made to empower.